This item circulating with
following damage:
THIS PAGE STAINED 4/12/22 Jw

Snakes

By Julie Guidone

Reading Consultant: Susan Nations, M.Ed.,
author/literacy coach/consultant in literacy development

WEEKLY READER®
PUBLISHING

Hussey-Mayfield Memorial
Zionsville IN 46077

Please visit our web site at **www.garethstevens.com**.
For a free catalog describing our list of high-quality books,
call 1-800-542-2595 (USA) or 1-800-387-3178 (Canada).
Our fax: 1-877-542-2596

Library of Congress Cataloging-in-Publication Data

Guidone, Julie.
 Snakes / by Julie Guidone.
  p. cm. — (Animals that live in the rain forest)
  Includes bibliographical references and index.
  ISBN-10: 1-4339-0027-0   ISBN-13: 978-1-4339-0027-3 (lib. bdg.)
  ISBN-10: 1-4339-0109-9   ISBN-13: 978-1-4339-0109-6 (softcover)
  1. Snakes—Juvenile literature. I. Title.
 QL666.O6G85   2009
 597.96—dc22   2008032241

This edition first published in 2009 by
Weekly Reader® Books
An Imprint of Gareth Stevens Publishing
1 Reader's Digest Road
Pleasantville, NY 10570-7000 USA

Copyright © 2009 by Gareth Stevens, Inc.

Executive Managing Editor: Lisa M. Herrington
Senior Editor: Barbara Bakowski
Creative Director: Lisa Donovan
Designers: Michelle Castro, Alexandria Davis
Photo Researcher: Diane Laska-Swanke
Publisher: Keith Garton

Photo Credits: Cover © Michael & Patricia Fogden/Minden Pictures; pp. 1, 19 © Piotr Naskrecki/
Minden Pictures; p. 5 © Gerry Ellis/Minden Pictures; p. 7 © Cheryl Ertelt/Visuals Unlimited, Inc.;
pp. 9, 17 (right), 21 © Pete Oxford/Minden Pictures; pp. 10-11 © Daniel Gomez/naturepl.com;
p. 13 © Steve Cooper/Photo Researchers, Inc.; p. 15 © Luciano Candisani/Minden Pictures;
p. 17 (left) © Papilio/Alamy

Printed in the United States of America

1 2 3 4 5 6 7 8 9 10 09 08

Table of Contents

Boldface words appear in the glossary.

In Water or Trees

Rain forests are warm, wet woodlands. They are home to some of the world's biggest snakes. A snake is a kind of animal called a **reptile**.

carpet python

Anacondas and emerald tree boas are snakes that live in rain forests in South America. Anacondas spend most of their time in rivers and lakes.

anaconda

Emerald tree boas live in trees near water. They wrap their bodies around the branches. These snakes rarely come down to the ground.

emerald tree boa

A Super-Sized Snake

The anaconda is long and heavy.

It is the heaviest snake in the world.

An anaconda can weigh
as much as four grown-ups!

The anaconda's eyes and **nostrils** are high on its head. The snake can see and breathe with the rest of its body underwater.

nostrils

The anaconda hunts at night. It kills its **prey** by drowning or squeezing the animal. After a big meal, an anaconda may not eat again for weeks!

fish

Hunting Up High

Emerald tree boas have green bodies with white zigzag stripes. The baby snakes have orange or red bodies with spots.

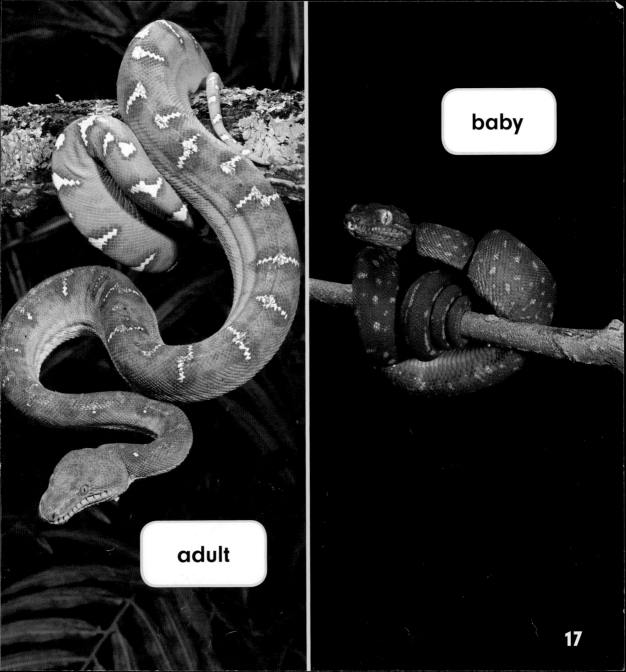

baby

adult

During the day, the emerald tree boa **coils** on a tree branch. The snake's colors help it hide. Its white stripes look like patches of sun on green leaves.

At night, the emerald tree boa looks for a meal. The snake uses its long teeth to catch small animals, such as birds, lizards, and frogs. Then it squeezes its prey and eats it whole!

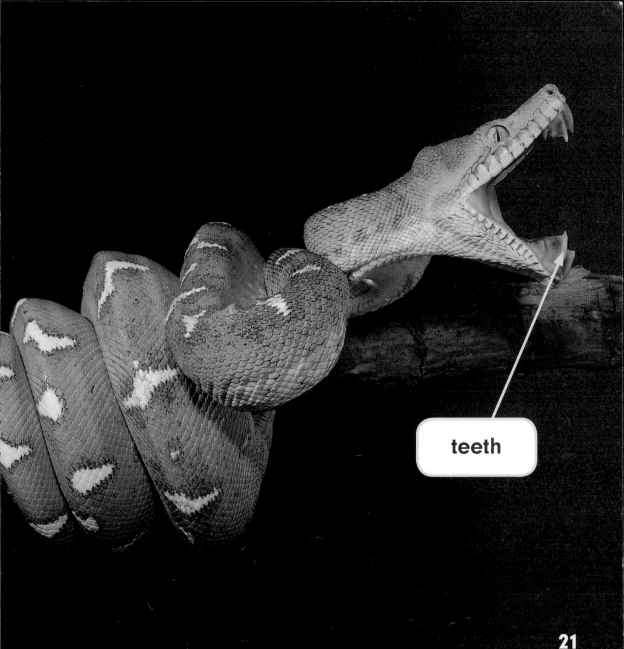

teeth

Glossary

coils: rolls or twists into loops or rings

nostrils: the pair of openings of the nose

prey: animals that are hunted and killed for food

rain forests: warm, rainy woodlands with many types of plants and animals

reptile: an animal that breathes air, has a backbone, and usually has scales or bony plates on its body, such as an alligator, a lizard, a snake, or a turtle

For More Information

Books

Amazing Snakes! I Can Read! (series). Sarah Thomson (Harper Trophy, 2006)

Green Anaconda: The World's Heaviest Snake. SuperSized! (series). Molly Smith (Bearport Publishing, 2007)

Web Sites

Creature Feature at National Geographic Kids
kids.nationalgeographic.com/Animals/CreatureFeature/Anaconda
Learn more about anacondas. See and hear the big snake as it slithers through water.

Lizards and Snakes Alive! Emerald and Amazonian Tree Boas
www.amnh.org/exhibitions/lizards/snakes/boas.php
This American Museum of Natural History site has fast facts and fun photos.

Index

About the Author

Julie Guidone has taught kindergarten and first and second grades in Madison, Connecticut, and Fayetteville, New York. She loves to take her students on field trips to the zoo to learn about all kinds of animals! She lives in Syracuse, New York, with her husband, Chris, and her son, Anthony.

24